Low
Fat
Raw
Vegan

Lifestyle Regeneration

Arnold N. Kauffman

Copyright © 2016 by Arnold N. Kauffman

All rights reserved. No part of this publication may be reproduced, distributed, or transmitted in any form or by any means, including photocopying, recording, or other electronic or mechanical methods, without the prior written permission of the publisher, except in the case of brief quotations embodied in critical reviews and certain other noncommercial uses permitted by copyright law. For permission requests, write to the publisher, addressed below.

Quantity sales: Special discounts are available on quantity purchases by corporations, associations, and others. For details, contact the publisher.

Orders by U.S. trade bookstores and wholesalers: Please contact Arnold's Way at

Arnold's Way

319 West Main Street

Suite #4

Lansdale, PA 19446.

Tel: (215)361-0116

For more information, visit www.arnoldsway.com

Or visit Arnold's Way on Youtube & Facebook

First Edition

Printed in the United States of America

ISBN 978-1535251952

Medical and Exercise Disclaimers

This book is not intended as a substitute for the medical advice of physicians. The reader should regularly consult a physician in matters relating to his or her health and particularly with respect to any symptoms that may require diagnosis or medical attention. The opinions expressed in this book are made by the author only, and the reader takes full responsibility for taking and using the advice provided herein.

The information in this book is meant to supplement, not replace, proper rebounder training. Like any sport involving speed, equipment, balance and environmental factors, rebounding poses some inherent risk. The author and publisher advise readers to take full responsibility for their safety and know their limits. Before practicing the skills described in this book, be sure your equipment is well-maintained. Do not take risks beyond your level of experience, aptitude, training and comfort level.

Table of Contents

Dedication 5

Foreword 6

The Way of Arnold 7

The Seven Stages of Disease 9

My Morning Routine 12

Words are Impressions onto the Cells . . . 18

The Raw Vegan Lifestyle 19

Fruit Diet for Rejuvenation 20

The Three Basic Requirements for Food before Eating . 22

Breakfast 23

Lunch 33

Dinner 39

My All-Time Favorite Dish 44

Sauce / Dips / Soup 45

Soup-to-Nuts Transition Guide to a Raw Food Diet . 48

Soups 50

Snacks and in-between 54

In conclusion… 55

DEDICATION

I dedicate this book to everyone who seeks the truth that's necessary to live a healthier lifestyle. This book seeks to fill your life with more joy, love and vibrancy to live a more passionate existence. Enjoy this unique recipe book! I hope that you find your path, I have found mine.

Foreword

My name is Arnold N. Kauffman and I am the owner of *Arnold's Way Raw Vegan Café* in Lansdale, PA. I wrote this book after I got motivated during the week of February 15–22, 2016. At that time, three men with brain health issues (inflammation, cancer, and lesions) approached me inquiring about an alternative option for their healing. All of them were given no hope by medical professionals other than the popular methods of chemotherapy and/or radiation. At the same time period, a lot of customers came into my raw vegan café seeking my alternative cancer healing remedy.

I have studied how to naturally heal diseases for over 25 years. I have literally seen hundreds of hopeless people sent home by their doctors. A simple change in their lifestyle, had them completely recovered and they are thriving to this day. We have had so many success stories over and over after they engaged in a serious lifestyle change. It is under these auspices that I begin directing my energy into creating a lifestyle/recipe book. As well as a new documentary recently released, titled "the power of raw" which focuses on people who were given no hope of recovering from their illnesses.

This book is the result of my 25+ years of experience confronting almost every illness or disease possible. I have seen hundreds of people who could not follow our LFRV* protocol. As well as those who have followed this LFRV* protocol and are thriving. The protocol is relatively easy and has remarkable results, it is not rocket science! It's just a simple and easy lifestyle change that will transform your life!

What you eat and don't eat is equally important. The goal is to make conscious food decisions for yourself. I strongly urge a lifestyle which focuses on low-fat, raw vegan food to create a transformation within one's own life successfully.

This book focuses on what is ideal, and more importantly, on how to have the mental and emotional strength to create optimal health for yourself and to those around you. All healing and rejuvenation are based on my theories, my opinion, my studies and my experience. Love is the most important part of healing and rejuvenation. "Every moment is a moment of Love"!

I dedicate this book to all those seeking a higher level of hope. Be inspired to join me as we: "Create an energetic movement for the transformation of a disease-free world".

Arnold N. Kauffman

*LFRV = Low Fat Raw Vegan

The Way of Arnold

Experiencing your full potential while turning back the clock with every loving raw moment

At 69, Arnold Kauffman, owner of the world-famous raw vegan café, *Arnold's Way*, shares what he's learned over 25 years of exploring how we can enhance our health and well-being through diet and exercise. Kaufman has been a raw vegan enthusiast since 1998, consuming mostly fruits and greens, and exercising almost daily.

A self-described 'lean, mean, fighting machine', but known as one of the most loving, and gentle human beings. Kauffman once operated a junk-food business. Upon inspiration when and where he least expected it, he closed the business to open Arnold's Way in 1992. Located outside of Philadelphia, Arnold's Way evolved from a vitamin and herb store to become a vegan café, and eventually a raw vegan café. Kauffman has educated thousands of his customers to eat raw food and transition to, mostly or wholly, raw lifestyles. He's also taught many on how they can reverse health challenges by creating optimum healing conditions for their bodies. In this book, Kauffman shares his wisdom and explains why his daily routine is The Way of Arnold.

This book features a moment-to-moment guide on how to eat and win the war against illness.

> *In my personal opinion, from what I have seen and experienced, there is no other answer out there. I have seen hundreds of cases where people are looking for an outer source, such as an herb, a supplement or a treatment. All of these options may seem logical; however without the basis of the 7 stages of healing, it will not work.*

Innate intelligence exists within the body, coded in the DNA, is the ability to repair itself and be in the best of health. The body can heal itself without the need of an alternative supplement or an herb. There is no magic pill. Every action and every movement is by the bodies design. The body operates at the highest healing energy without mistakes, and is genetically designed to all heal by itself. The body is designed "to rock and role till the day you die"—AK

*AK = Arnold Kauffman

> *Our body's continuous goal is purification and homeostasis.*

The Basics

The following is what I give to every customer who has a health issue, whether depression, colitis, migraine or even brain cancer. I composed it over 6 years. This was based on my dealings with customers, for over 10 years who sought an easy solution to deal with whatever was ailing them, without going the traditional medical route. It's based on the body's design to deal with the overload of toxic debris that is circulating in the system, and when the body is at a point of not being able to operate at 100% efficiency, it enters into healing crises.

Beginning with the 7 stages of healing—notice Love is the first factor—and the most important one. Even if a person is doing everything correct, eating right, sleeping enough, and exercising almost daily, there is still a problem. If someone is in either a bad relationship, bad job and not in a loving caring supportive environment, it won't work. The key is Love.

7 Steps to Optimal Health

Remove the cause of the disease and the body will do whatever it can to self-heal.

- **LOVE:** our body understands thoughts. Every Moment is a Moment of Love.
- **SPECIES-SPECIFIC DIET:** composed mostly of fruits, which are easy to digest, and leafy greens, which can be juiced, blended or eaten whole.
- **EXERCISE:** vigorous exercise is best in the morning, 3–5 times per week.
- **SLEEP:** is best 2–3 hours before midnight and 3 hours after dinner, for a total of 7–8 hours, minimum.
- **FRESH AIR and SUNSHINE:** 20 minutes per day. Ideally before 11am or after 3pm.
- **WATER:** drink as needed, preferably not during meals.
- **FASTING:** 12 hours daily, ideally from 7pm to 7am, and better if longer.

4 Factors to Determine the Best Food for Health

The majority of what we eat should be:

- Grown in nature
- Found on a tree, bush or vine in its raw, organic state
- Yummy to the tummy
- Combined appropriately for optimal digestion

2 Reasons We Stay Healthy

- **KNOWLEDGE:** taking total responsibility for our health and taking responsibility for our health and educating ourselves.
- **CONSCIOUSNESS:** becoming aware and trusting our innate healing abilities and proactively supporting them.

The Seven Stages of Disease

The body reacts to the accumulation of toxic materials causing it to get sick. The body's continuous goal is purification and homeostasis. The accumulation of toxic materials is called toxemia or toxicosis.

1
- **ENERVATION OR NERVOUS SYSTEM EXHAUSTION:** The condition of imbalance in the ratio of available body energy relative to the nerve energy available for necessary task performance. This creates a gradual, physical and/or moral weakening which, if not corrected, continues to worsen and further debilitate the organism. Sleep is restorative to the nervous system (energy for the nervous system—if you will) as quality food energizes the rest of the body. *The best way to restore nerve energy is to sleep.*

2
- **TOXICOSIS:** If the body doesn't have the energy to eliminate toxic substances, the blood and tissues, the lymph system and interstitial fluids become imbued. The toxic materials may be generated exogenously, i.e. originating from outside the body, such as through poor food choices, topically applied toxins or inhaled toxins; or they may be generated endogenously, i.e. originating from inside the body, as in the case of cellular metabolic debris. *It is important to discontinue unhealthy practices at this stage; otherwise the body will begin to experience irritation.*

3
- **IRRITATION:** The result of the nervous system detecting an over-abundance of toxic material. This may manifest as an itch, sneeze, feeling queasy, jumpy, antsy, irritable, arousal, bodily urges, or general annoyance. This irritation is a prodding from the nervous system signaling distress. This prodding is saying "take heed", for if the causes of toxic materials are not discontinued, cleared out and the body rested, the body will then introduce the next sate of the disease: inflammation.

4 • **INFLAMMATION:** A local response to toxemia and injury on a cellular level characterized by capillary dilation, leukocytic infiltration, redness, heat, fever, and/or pain as a mechanism to start the elimination of noxious agents and/or damage tissue. Although the pain and redness is the body's natural attempt to resolve the challenge, and what the body needs is to be rested and detoxified, because of the pain and suffering present, the sufferer usually contacts a physician at this stage. Unfortunately, the assistance usually given is something that suppresses the cleaning process and further thwarts the body's natural healing processes. Medications further increase the amount of toxins in the body.

5 • **ULCERATION:** Characterized by mucous membrane or tissue breakdown, with disintegration and necrosis (dying) of tissue, often followed by the formation of pus. This is often painful since the nerves may be exposed. The body creates this condition in order to alleviate itself from an over-abundance of toxic material. Excessive build-up of toxins necessitates extreme measures to cleanse. After this has been accomplished with the cause of the toxicity removed, the body will repair the wound.

6 • **INDURATION:** Characterized by a hardening and filling in of empty space, created by the destroyed tissue, with fibrous elements known as scarring and encapsulation. This process of encapsulation engulfs the toxic materials in a gelatinous, hardened fibrous sac in order to isolate them from the rest of the body. This is commonly referred to as tumor formation. This is the last intelligent thing the body will do in an effort to protect vital organs before the last and final stage of disease.

7 • **FUNGATION OR CANCER:** Mutation and proliferation of cells. The cells and tissues go awry due to the disruption of their genetic coding by the poisonous toxins. These mutated cells obtain their nourishment from lymph fluid but do not serve the body, as if they have forgotten their heritage as human cells with an agenda independent and without regard to the rest of the body. Although this stage is often final, if the causes of the pathology are discontinued, the possibility of cleansing, repair and rehabilitation still exists. Remove the cause; give the body a healthy, healing condition!

What causes a disease? What to do if sick?

There are presently thousands of known diseases in the medical world. In my world, there is only one disease, *toxicosis*. *Toxicosis* is the bodies reaction to the accumulation of toxic materials. As soon as food is cooked above 115°F, the basic components are destroyed, making it useless to the body. When enough toxic build-up occurs, the body has to act accordingly to expel it successfully. In the 7 stages of disease, each phase of toxic removal increases in urgency up until the last stage, which is fungation or cancer. The body takes steps all along the way to handle these excess toxins.

In the medical world, there are thousands of medicines, supplements, herbs, tests and treatments for every disease. However, in my world, everything is based on natural hygiene. Hygiene is the science of healing and protecting itself from harmful interferences or invasions, both internally and externally.

In the medical world, the basic assumption is that medicine is given the innate knowledge of where to go — navigating through 98,000 miles of arteries and once it arrives at the destination, it knows how to correct and destroy anything harmful to the body. What people do not understand is that medicine has no RNA, no DNA and is not even considered food. Using this as a basis, how is the body going to heal itself by taking any medicine if the body cannot recognize it? From my understanding, food that the body can use has to meet 6 requirements, in order for digestion or usage to occur.

Following are the six requirements for the body to recognize and digest food source:

Glucose:
as our energy supply

Protein:
building structure for the body

Fatty acid/oil:
making hormones

Vitamins:
Minerals (Vitamins and minerals work together to help our body work more efficiently)

Water:
every metabolic process that happens in the body requires it

Medicine and herbs (in pill or oil form) do not meet any of the six requirements mentioned above. But it seems medicine, herbs (in pill form) and supplements do work. It appears, in my opinion, that the body's healing process has to stop in order to attempt to recognize and deal with the foreign substance it is being involuntarily invaded with. It means the body is no longer in a healing crisis because it has a more important agenda to destroy the invasive substance which presents a greater harm to itself. Therefore, anything that does not meet these six requirements is a distraction to proper healing.

A doctor will not prescribe any medicine or antibiotic to a healthy person. You cannot go to a doctor and ask for an antibiotic or a steroid, thinking it will make you healthier, fit or happier. The doctor will refuse to give you any medicine for a healthier purpose, based on their understanding that any medicine given to a healthy person would make them sick. Applying this same logic, the same medication supposedly makes a sick person healthier. This makes absolutely no sense to me.

My Morning Routine

Sleep deprivation is one of the reasons why a person gets sick. In my case, I have arranged my bedroom into a place conducive to sleeping. To give you an idea of how my bedroom looks like, the following are the changes I did:

The Bedroom:

- Filled with plants for oxygen.
- Window open.
- No clutter.
- The bedroom looking like it's ready for a guest.
- Clean inside and out.
- No computer or cell phone next to the bed. Ideally, no alarm clock.

Optional:

- Salt lamp for air cleansing.
- Water fountain for relaxation.

My morning routine, which I do 3-4 times a week, has helped me also become physically, emotionally and mentally tough.

Power Stance

I continually do the power stance throughout the day. A power stance is simply standing, a way that makes me feel like I am in charge and ready to take on anything. I have my hands on my hips and my legs slightly spread apart (shoulder width). Standing straight with a good posture, core tucked in and chest out, with fists clenched is how I stand to show my power. This power stance helps in me be being mentally tough and ready for any given situation. When one is mentally and emotionally alert, diet changes come easy.

Having a mantra is also an important part of setting a healthy mindset. It is an important key element in every health transformation. A mantra is something you strive to become — a phrase you say every day to reinforce your own power. What you believe is what you become. For example, my mantra is "lean, mean, fighting machine" and this is what I aspire to become. By repeating this daily, I embrace the reputation for myself and I approach my day from a point of power and inner strength.

> *The way you carry yourself changes the way you see yourself.*

Super Brain Yoga

To make the most of your brain, it must be exercised and nurtured regularly just as any other muscle in the body. Synapses, or points of brain connections, must be created and conserved for the brain's optimal function. By utilizing super brain yoga, the right and left hemispheres of the brain come into synchronicity. Once trapped, this energy can flow freely to the bodies energy centers and create a calm sense, inner peace, and mental clarity. It will also help improve your decision-making ability.

The following is a super brain yoga exercise that I religiously observed:

- Take your left hand and grab your right earlobe, thumb in front; then cross your right arm over to grab your left earlobe, also with the thumb in front.

- Make sure your left arm is close to your chest and inside your right arm.

- Press your tongue against the roof of your mouth.

- Inhale through your nose and squat.

- Repeat this up to 40 times.

- Remember to keep squeezing your earlobes the entire time.

Vision Board

A vision board is an important tool in visualizing your future. It helps you manifest the things you want the most. A vision board is a collage of images and phrases that inspire you. By putting your dreams and aspirations on the board, you are taking your thoughts and making them an instant reality. For example, you wish to save up enough money to move to Hawaii. On your board, you might have pictures of a tropical home, fruit trees, the ocean and motivational quotes to help you get there. Your thoughts become your reality, when you create a vision board for yourself. I highly recommend this to anyone seeking a better future.

Breathing Technique

My ideal breathing technique is deep and long breaths through my stomach that go through my nose with my mouth closed, so that I am using 100% of my lungs capacity. When you breathe with your open mouth and shoulders moving, there is no total body oxygenation. Shallow breathing contributes to anxiety and lack of energy. It causes many other health issues as well.

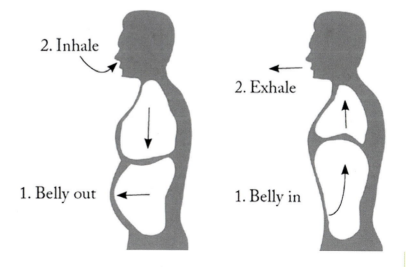

Self-Massage

Different parts of the body are tied to coinciding internal organs and emotions. By massaging the proper areas, we can relax the body and induce healing. I do this every morning as a sign of love, of empowerment, and of being in charge. I have made 2 videos for you. to demonstrate how I do my daily self-massage so you can learn how to do it too. Visit the Arnold's Way YouTube Channel and search "self-massage" or follow the links below.

https://youtu.be/cL92uWyXo5M   https://youtu.be/L738f4iepTQ

To continually have the best day ever, one has to reinforce his self-image. Saying key words to yourself like, "super-duper excellent", "you are the greatest", or whatever words work best for you, you can never have a bad day.

Tapping

Tapping is a practice based on the belief that the body never forgets. Traumas from the past, even as far back as childhood, can still affect our level of health today. By repeating a mantra of self-love while tapping on certain trigger points of the body, we can release the pain that is no longer serving us and heal whatever physical ailment was being caused by the repression.

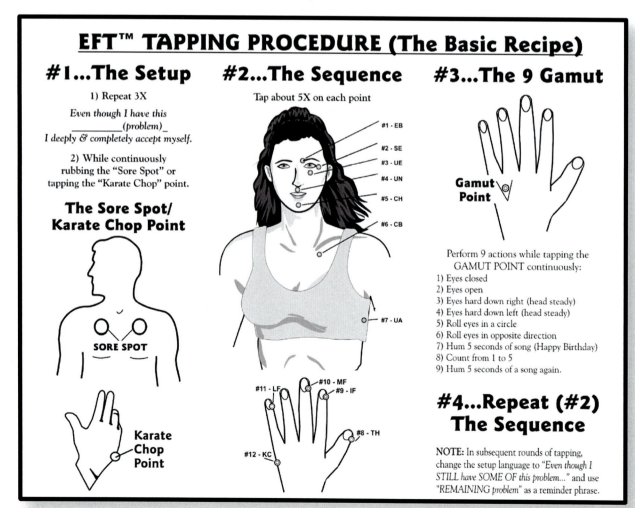

Don't Count Calories and Carb Up!

You've heard it before, the *"calories in, calories out"* method of weight loss. This method suggests that all calories are created equal — a person can be just as fit and healthy eating 2,000 calories of ice cream and soda as a person who consumes 2,000 calories of fruits and vegetables. I'm here to tell you this is rubbish! The body needs the right amount of calories to function, an array of essential vitamins and minerals, and glucose (which comes from carbs) for energy. Your body knows best. Starving yourself, that is not eating; when you feel hungry, in order to lose a few pounds, creates distrust in your body. Eventually your body will force you to make up for missing nutrients by triggering a binge on the most calorie-dense food it can remember. This is the reason why calorie counting never works long term. You will always rebound. However, by listening to your body's hunger signals and continually providing it with nutritionally and energetically dense foods such as fruits and vegetables, it will love you back and the weight will simply fall off effortlessly! If listening to your best friend creates a mutually trusting relationship, so does listening to your body.

The Sun

The sun expels a much-underrated nutrient (Vitamin D) every cell in our body requires it. Once health becomes a focus, one will do whatever it takes to become more attuned to life's rhythm. During cold climates like winter, I always take walks outside in the park. I even purposefully park my car further away in the lot, when going to my store. Whenever possible, I always try to go to the park. I also have received loads of oxygen, through plants inside my house.

All these processes should take no more than 10 minutes in the morning, constantly reinforcing your self-image.

Words are Impressions onto the Cells

Your Cells Understand English

An invigorating feeling is ideal. When you say words like "super-duper" or "excellent", you feel so invigorated. These words are also very impressionable to the cells. Cells understand the energy behind words, so the intention is very important as well. When my intentions and words are of good energy, I can never have a bad day.

Exercise

I exercise in the morning on an empty stomach and after being well-rested. A satisfactory amount of sleep is 7–8 hours for me. After I wake up, I begin my warm up routine for the day. After the warm up, I am ready to rock and roll! The longer my exercise is, the better I feel. I avoid evening exercise, as it leads to weight loss. If I do not exercise in the morning on any given day, I do not exercise that day. My house is my workout area and I do not need a gym. There is no need for traveling, and I have more time to focus on myself.

My key piece of workout equipment is a *rebounder*.

Rebounding is described as the best exercise for the lymph system. There were so many testimonies on natural cancer survival that mentioned jumping on a mini trampoline, also known as Rebounding.

Rebounding is a form of exercise that creates an increased gravitational load that positively stresses every cell in our body. Because of these forces, our entire musculoskeletal system is strengthened. Our bones, muscles, connective tissues and even organs are stimulated thereby resulting to a healthier you.

Rebounding has been my rock exercise for about 20 years. I literally live and die by this form of exercise as my foundation before anything else. The main reason I enjoy doing this exercise and strongly advocate it is because it helps keep the lymphatic system moving, and this process boosts the immune system. Doing this exercise keeps the body young. Rebounding works on three levels:

Acceleration (of word of motion)

Deceleration (downward motion)

Gravitational (downward pull)

When these three parts are joined in a single plane, the lymph system begins a pumping action to remove all waste that surrounds each cell. When this happens, the immune system has more room to move, and when it moves, it will attack any cell that is not part of the body, especially cancer cells. These cancer cells are destroyed by one immune fighter in particular, the T8 Cell, which contains hydrogen peroxide. This agent kills all cancer cells that it zaps.

I generally workout at home, anywhere from 30 minutes to 2 hours, 3-4 times weekly. I have my daily workout routine, which at the age of 69, it keeps getting better and better.

The Raw Vegan Lifestyle

The raw vegan lifestyle with a focus on fruit is so amazingly easy! As you continue reading, you will begin to understand this is not just an ordinary recipe book. It is much more than that.

This is my way of sharing 25 years of personal experience. My continuing goal is to be in a state of exuberant vibrancy with every breath to be in a state of rocking and rolling, no matter what!

I am literally inspired to share my words when six people afflicted with cancer approached me a few months back seeking for my help. Three were men with brain lesions or cancer. Jerry, one of the men, was advised by his doctor that his sickness is a hopeless case and to get his papers in order for he has only 6 months to live.

This is a cause for us to be alarmed. Our bodies are being overrun by our poor dietary choices like processed food and meat, along with so many chemical additives. Unless we do something to arrest this problem, our body will continue to self-destruct.

It is on this note that I am compelled to do whatever it takes to reverse this seemingly unstoppable force that is gripping the minds and souls of so many. I write this lifestyle book for that reason. I've seen the light and walked through the darkness. I have experienced the pain of many who failed. I have seen those who succeeded and overcome their serious illness. They shined and became lights for the others.

Fruit Diet for Rejuvenation

I promote mostly a fruit diet with focus on low-fat raw vegan food. These recipes are simple and easy to remember. The ingredients are found in any supermarket and do not need specific amounts. You can adjust the amount of each ingredient as you wish.

The recipes found in this book are used as the basis for changing your lifestyle towards a healthier you. This book is a stepping stone to reach your goal of achieving optimal health by maintaining a dietary regimen like mine.

On an average day, I consume the following fruits in this order:

- **My Green Smoothie, approx. 30 ounces (breakfast 10am-noon)**
  - 5-7 bananas
  - 1 apple
  - 1 pear
  - 2 oz dates
  - 8 – 12 oz water

- **Guacamole (lunch, noon-4pm)**
  - 2 Avocados
  - 2–3 stalks of Celery
  - 1 Tomato
  - 1/2 of a Cucumber
  - Juice of 1 Lemon

- **Banana Whip (dinner, 4pm–6pm)**
  - 5 Bananas
  - 2 oz. of Dates
  - Desired amount of Carob

I also graze on watermelon, blackberries, blueberries, and other fruits in season until 6pm, when I generally stop eating. Three to four days a week, this is my routine.

And for those who want a pure diet, you can have the following as substitutes:

- Substitute cacao with carob.
- Substitute granola with a mixture of dehydrated flaxseed, buckwheat, apple, pear, and dates.
- Substitute maple syrup with blended dates and water.
- Substitute Braggs Liquid Aminos or Nama Shoyu with coconut aminos or, optimally, lemon juice.

But do eliminate:

- Irritants such as salt, ginger, spices, garlic and onion.
- Oil.

I am primarily living on a fruit diet. I love it. This lifestyle keeps me young and almost ageless. I haven't aged much since I started it 17 years ago.

The Three Basic Requirements for Food before Eating

The question remains "what food to eat?" By my definition, here is what a real food is compared to a junk food. There are three basic requirements for choosing the right food to eat.

Was the food grown in nature?

This means that anything that nature provides can be eaten provided it meets the following two requirements.

Was the food found on a tree, bush, vine or on the ground?

Once again, nature is, by design, for our benefit. It does not need to be improved upon. It is perfect in its natural form, having the energy of the sun, moon, earth, and the water, all of which contain the universal power of life, which has taken millions of years to perfect.

Is the food yummy to the tummy?

This is a key element to this lifestyle. This is what separates the men from the boys, what separates truth from lies, what is good for our bodies to eat and what is not. There is no gray area and no questions whether it's good or bad for our body. If one cannot eat anything in a large quantity that is raw, ripe and fresh from the garden, it means we are not genetically designed to eat it. We need to remember that all kinds of oil, which are 100% fat, and all salts, which are very unhealthy in small quantities, should never be eaten. Garlic, which causes our mouths to spit up like a bad dream, should never be eaten. The same goes for all condiments like pepper, ginger or any spice, which supposedly "enhances" the flavor of food but sets our body to go on full-scale military alerts to neutralize and eliminate these condiments.

These are the rules of life. There is neither middle ground nor any gray areas. Our body thrives on being in a state of perfection and harmony. Any food or recipe ingredient we put into our mouths has to meet these requirements, so it can be enjoyed. Keep in mind that I am talking about following this practice in an ideal world; that wherever you are in the big scheme of things, enjoy your life; and that self-love ranks the highest order. Food represents a part of the picture. It's a big part, but not the whole picture.

For me, breakfast and dinner are the most important meals. As such, they must meet these requirements. Initially, lunch can be a cheat meal, but I recommend that you eat a salad just before you ingest these cheat meals. A salad will fill you up and make you less prone to binge on cooked food. In the long-term, you will lose the desire for cheat meals as your body will demand excellence in its diet. If you stray toward cooked and complicated fare, enjoy it and then get back on track the next day so your body can catch up.

Breakfast

Food is the key for rejuvenation and detoxification. The simpler, the better. It's all about calorie and nutrient rich food, utilizing less energy on digestion.

Earn Your Breakfast

I am a strong believer in "earning your breakfast". I learned that from Paul Bragg, who passed away at the age of 98 while surfboarding in the ocean. My first meal is between 9–10am and I generally stop eating between 5–7pm (usually around 6pm).

ONLY Fruit Until Noon!

Fruit requires no digestive energy. The less energy there is on digestion, the more energy is put towards the body's healing.

Elimination within the body takes place according to natural or circadian rhythms from the hours of 4am till noon. Ideally, it is best to eat only one fruit at a time. It is good to load up on fruit-based carbohydrates with 700–1000 calories, at each meal. Nutrient-rich foods do not need digestive energy. Fruit is both nutrient- and calorie-rich and has plenty of glucose which fuels every cell. This explains why fruit is best until noon.

What to eat and what not to eat? It is not what you think.

Fruit is the key! Fruit has calories, fuel, and nutrients; while vegetables don't have calories aka fuel.

- 1 pound of vegetables has 100 calories.
- The average person needs 2000-3000 daily calories.
- The Green Smoothie is my rock!
- Arnold's Green Smoothie
- 1 Apple (cored)
- 1 Pear (cored)
- 3 leaves of Collard Greens or Kale
- 2-6 Bananas
- 2-4 Dates
- Fill the blender halfway with water.

Ideally, the bananas should be at room temperature.

This smoothie has anywhere from 600-1000 calories. Calorie needs are based on your lifestyle and activity!

To get a calorie requirement, calculate your weight multiplied by 10 to get your BMR. If I did absolutely nothing all day, with my weight at 140 lbs., I would need 1400 calories to do my bodily function for the day.

If I had a super active lifestyle, I would need an extra 800-1000 calories per day. I typically need 400-600 additional calories, per day.

Breakfast can be switched up with different smoothies. In the beginning, it is best not to worry about food combinations, unless digestive issues are present.

Acid Fruits

Blackberry, grapefruit, lemon, lime, orange, pineapple, strawberry, tomato

Sub-acid Fruits

Apple, apricot, blueberry, cherry, fresh fig, kiwi, mango, nectarine, papaya, peach, plum

Sweet Fruits

Banana, dates, dried fruit, dry fig, persimmon

Melons

- Watermelon, honeydew, cantaloupe

Add more or less water, or if you want to splurge, use raw coconut water. Sweet fruit contains the most calories.

Banana Stacks

- ½ cup of Mixed Berries
- 3 Bananas
- 2–3 chopped Dates
- *Optional: add Cinnamon

Banana Stacks with Coconut Sprinkles and Carob Date Sauce

The Champion Juicer is my savior for breakfast!
Almost daily, I have the recipe listed below!

Arnold's Signature Banana Whip

- 1 tablespoon of Carob
- 2–3 frozen Bananas
- 1–2 Dates

- Put the bananas, carob and dates through the Champion juicer all together!
- It's like heaven rolled into a bowl!

The two previous meal suggestions can be changed into thousands of combinations! In the succeeding pages, you will find a fruit mixing chart where you can mix, match or double the amount of fruits, depending on how hungry you are. Use your imagination as there are no mistakes. This is about whatever you like, and that's the key!

These recipes can be blended, chopped in a food processor, added to a bowl of lettuce, or put through a Champion Juicer with frozen fruits. Add coconut for variety or whatever toppings you choose!

These fruit recipes are great for detoxification and rejuvenation. By using these fruit recipes or any fruit of your choice, the body will do whatever it takes to heal itself.

The Hawaiian Piña Colada

- 1/4 cup of Coconut flakes
- 1/2 cup of Mango
- 1/2 cup of Pineapple
- 2 frozen of Bananas
- 2-3 Dates

*Sprinkle desired amount of Coconut Flakes on

Piña Colada Banana Whip with Carob Date Sauce

Fill the blender halfway with water and add the rest! This is calorie and nutrient rich! The taste is beyond good and it is so good for you!

Piña Colada Banana Whip

- 1/2 cup frozen Mango
- 1/2 cup frozen Pineapple
- 2-3 frozen Bananas
- 2 Dates

Banana whips and smoothies are great for breakfast, or can be enjoyed at any particular time of the day depending on your preferences.

- Banana, Mango, Date Pudding
- 2-3 Bananas
- 1 Mango
- 4 Dates

Mix all of these ingredients in the food processor until smooth and serve immediately.

Carob Date Sauce

- 1/4 cup of Date paste
- 1/4 cup of Roasted or raw Carob (optimal)
- 2-3 Bananas

Add enough water to desired consistency.

Place all of these ingredients into a blender and mix. This sauce will knock your socks off!

This is easy to make and is great to add to any banana whip or fruit dish.

Mango-Papaya Pudding

- 2 Bananas
- 1 Mango
- 1 Papaya
- 3 Dates

Place all ingredients into the food processor and mix until smooth.

Remember: breakfast should only be fruits. Green smoothies are the key to success. There are so many choices to choose from. Breakfast possibilities are endless!

The 5 S's:
Soup
Salad
Sauce
Smoothie
Stuffed

All these breakfast recipes can also be taken during lunch or dinner, or even in-between meals! In an ideal world, fruit is the best choice as it is nutrient rich and do not require a lot of energy to digest!

All meals can be interchanged, so 5 ingredients can be transformed over and over.

Add banana whips to the mixture and you have a different breakfast each day of the year, for the rest of your life. There's no need for medications and doctor; your pain will go away by consuming plenty of fruits each day.

At the time this book is printed, I am 69. I am rocking and rolling like I am still 25 years young.

Carob Pudding

- 2 Bananas
- 2 Dates
- 2 tablespoons of Carob
- Desired amount of raisins

Place all ingredients into a food processor and mix. Keep in mind that this should all be guesswork to you. If you want more of some ingredients or less of other ingredients, there are no mistakes. This is all about you when you prepare this food and your taste preferences should be achieved through the making of this food.

Carob Date Pudding

For large parties or potlucks, the meal below is my go-to meal. It is quick and easy!

Frozen Carob Pie

Use a 6-inch deep rectangular container, width and length are dependent on the desired amount. Place cut bananas at the bottom. Place the carob pudding on top of the bananas until well-covered. Put it in the freezer.

Apple Pear Delight

- 1 Apple
- 1 Pear
- 1/2 cup of Coconut Flakes
- 2-3 Dates
- *Optional, add raisins and cinnamon

Place all ingredients into a food processor and pulse until chunky or smooth, whichever you prefer.

Apple Pear Delight

Remember the 5S theory, with bananas whips as your backup. Mix and match as you please. Your choices are unlimited! The taste is beyond magnificent.

The 5 theory
5 Ingredients
5 Dollars
5 Minutes

This makes life so easy, and any meal can be made using this philosophy! This philosophy includes fruit that is fresh and yummy to the tummy.

Super Berry Smoothie

- 1 cup of Berries (your choice)
- 2-3 frozen Bananas
- 2-3 Dates
- 1 teaspoon of Acai powder
- 1/2 cup of Coconut Water

Place all ingredients into a blender and blend until smooth. This recipe can be used as a sauce, as well, to pour over fruit. You can also switch the recipe up with other fruits.

> "Fruit is the simplest, easiest, cost effective, time efficient and the most delicious way to optimal health"
> Arnold N. Kauffman

Smoothies are an easy way to get your caloric needs. They are masticated, so there is no need to chew on so much fruit throughout the day. They are the fastest and the easiest way to fulfill your daily calorie requirements. Another benefit from smoothies is that they are easy to carry around and do not require much time to prepare.

Mono Mevals

Mono meal as the name implies is one food at a time. They are very healthy, tasty and colorful. Mono meals are excellent for healing since the digestive system is more efficient at receiving one calorie rich and nutrient dense fruit at a time, enabling the body more time to focus on detoxification and rejuvenation.

Mono meals are great meals any time of the day—breakfast, lunch or dinner! They are the best option for healing!

Mono Meals:
Are great for breakfast!
Are great for lunch!
Are great for dinner!
Are great as a snack!

Choose your favorite fruit!

Select your favorite fruit and just eat it one at a time. One 15 lb. watermelon is equivalent to 2100 calories. That is equivalent to a meal and is very simple as there is almost no preparation time involved! Just cut the watermelon into pieces. Eat it and enjoy!

Mono Fruits and their Caloric Amounts

0.8 lbs. of raisins	1200 calories
2 pineapples	1200 calories
8–10 pears	1200 calories
4 large bunches of Grapes	1250 calories
2 Cantaloupes	1200 calories
Bananas (10–13 medium)	1200 calories
Blueberries (4–lbs.)	1100 calories
Cherries (10 lbs.)	1150 calories
Dates (16 oz.)	1200 calories
Durian (1 large)	1350 calories
Figs (3.5 lbs.)	1150 calories
Mangos (6–8 medium)	1200 calories
Oranges (12–20 medium)	1200 calories
Papayas (3–5 medium)	1200 calories
Persimmons (7–8 medium)	1200 calories
Raspberries (8–9 pints)	1200 calories
Strawberries (8 lbs.)	1200 calories

All of these quantities may seem expensive and overwhelming. The quantities are also almost impossible to eat unless blended. When blended, this becomes very easy to consume.

Lunch

Lunch is my heaviest meal, and like clockwork, I gravitate towards eating avocado mostly. I eat 2 avocados for lunch, daily.

I believe lunch should be the heaviest meal. I always choose to have avocados during lunch. Avocados are 65% fat while nuts are 80% fat. I rarely choose nuts.

The same holds true for olive oil that goes on top of salads, it is 100% fat. I sometimes eat guacamole as a lunch substitute.

Lunch Possibilities Applying the 5'S and 5-5-5 Theories

The following recipes are lunch possibilities. Keep in mind that there are no mistakes. All the ingredients are in the whole form, have not been packaged, processed, fried, baked, or steamed. Each ingredient is loaded with the essential nutrients that can be used by the body, as intended by nature.

Summer Jubilee

- ½ shredded Beet
- ½ shredded Carrot
- 1 Apple

This recipe can be made as a salad, sauce, soup or a smoothie.

If this recipe is made as a salad, it can be placed over a bed of greens. For more calories, add some avocado to this recipe.

Tropical Sauce

- 1 Pineapple
- 1 Mango

Place all of the ingredients in the food processor, and blend until smooth. Pour this over the summer jubilee.

If the summer jubilee is made as a smoothie or sauce, blend all of the ingredients together. Add 1 whole avocado for thickness, calories, and creaminess. Also, add lemon juice, and/or any other ingredients you like.

Spaghetti

Use beet, carrot, cucumber, daikon, parsnip, or zucchini.

You will need a spiralizer. The amount depends on how hungry you are.

I personally use zucchini for time-saving purposes. Zucchini is readily available. It is easy to work with, fairly inexpensive and most important, very tasty.

Low Fat Sauce/Salsa

- 2–3 Tomatoes
- 1 Sundried Tomato
- 1 Red Pepper
- ¼ cup Mango
- 2 Dates

Optional: Celery for crunch.

Place all of the ingredients in the food processor and pulse until chunky.

Other options with the sauce/salsa are to turn it into a soup or put it on a bed of lettuce as a salad. The sauce can also have more tomatoes or mangos, to better accommodate personal tastes.

- Jesse Nori Roll
- ½ of a Cucumber
- 1 Banana
- ¼ Red Bell Pepper
- 1 tablespoon Hemp Seeds

Slice the cucumber, banana and red pepper thin. Place these ingredients on the nori sheet, with lettuce roll the nori.

Zucchini Orzo

Use beet, carrot, cucumber, daikon, parsnip, or zucchini.

I use zucchini.

The amount depends on how hungry you are. The zucchini is shredded in a food processor.

Orzo Sauce

- Juice of 1 Lemon
- 2 Tomatoes
- ¼ Celery stalk
- 1 Avocado

Place this over the orzo or with whatever vegetables that you like.

Each recipe can be changed in hundreds of ways. There are no mistakes. The hardest part to understand is feeling the love!

- Kale Salad
- Simple! Kale without stems!
- Kale Salad Dressing
- 1 Avocado
- Juice of 1 Lemon
- 1 Sundried Tomato
- ½ cup of Water

Blend all of the ingredients together.

Add lettuce if you desire, and pour the dressing over the kale. Tomato and red pepper can be added for more color and variety.

The same ingredients can be used as a salad, sauce or a dip. You can add different vegetables, for different tastes and possibilities. For this recipe as a soup or smoothie, add less water and more celery, tomato, and greens making it rich green.

For the salad, add shredded lettuce, tomato, carrot, and celery. Add 1–1.5 avocados for calories.

Avocados should be eaten from 12–4pm ideally with no other fat.

> *"Too much fat prolongs digestion and reduces our body's ability to uptake, transport and deliver oxygen to trillions of cells. This causes fatigue, sluggishness and lack of clarity."*
>
> 80–10–10 Diet by Dr. Doug Graham page 129

Stuffed Tomatoes, Red Peppers or Mushrooms (you decide!)

Filling: just add dates and tahini. Place this in the food processor.

Use either and/or tomatoes, red peppers or mushrooms.

Tahini and dates are both rich in calories, which are necessary to fill you up. This will prevent you from binging. Eat until satisfied. Dates and tahini are not an ideal combination, yet are way better than the Standard American Diet. Keep in mind that proper food combination is ideal; however, food is not the only factor. Lifestyles, actions, environment and sleep also play a role in our healthier well-being. Just enjoy the journey!

Original Wrap

- 1-2 Tomatoes
- 1/2 cup of Carrots
- 2-3 stalks of Celery
- 1 Avocado
- ½ cup of Zucchini

Pulse all of the ingredients in the food processor.

To make 1 meal, place it in lettuce or collard green as a wrap. Or you can place it in nori as a wrap too.

You can add lemon juice to this recipe as well.

As always, use the 5'S theory for other meal options.

I use 1-2 avocados daily for calories. The avocado supplies the bulk of calories. Tomato, zucchini, and lemon are fruits; however, they have fewer calories than other fruits.

In my opinion, avocado, nuts or cooked food is what I recommend for lunch always.

> **Key points for lunch:**
> It should be the heaviest meal of the day.
> I graze on food heavily from 12–4pm.
> 4–6pm is my slowing down on food.
> I also begin preparing for the next day.

Lunch could either be nuts (no more than a handful) or avocados (1-2 daily). Each avocado has 250-500 calories. Each avocado is 65% fat, although it is considered a fruit. If you want to have cooked food, have it during lunch. Do not eat cooked food during breakfast or dinner. Cooked food, nuts, and seeds slow down detoxification. In the early stages of detoxification, you don't want to overload the kidneys or liver. Slow but sure is best for detoxification to be successful.

In a real healing crisis like cancer, multiple sclerosis or adrenal fatigue, start a transition to low-fat raw vegan lifestyle right away, with a focus on fruit.

The body can heal itself given the proper healing conditions. A key component to healing is fruit intake, which fuels every cell in our body and requires less energy on digestion.

Dinner

Ideally, dinner should be low in fat and should be fruit or vegetable based. The reason is that digestion needs less energy and, in turn the body more focused on energy for the body to heal. We should take dinner 3-4 hours before going to sleep.

In other words, dinner should be:

> **No fat**
> **No nuts**
> **No oil**
> **No spices**

By 5-6pm, aim for getting most of your calories. Dinner should be your lightest meal. After dinner, stop eating.

If you get hungry at night that means you did not eat enough during the day. Eating lots of fruits during the day will give you sufficient calories and carbohydrates. One of the best ways to get your daily caloric intake is through smoothies.

The Basics of Food Combining

Food combining is based on love—one God, one love, one food. Our bodies have a hard time dealing with complex meals. This is the reason why I recommend eating one fruit at a time (mono meal). Meat, dairy, and processed foods should be avoided.

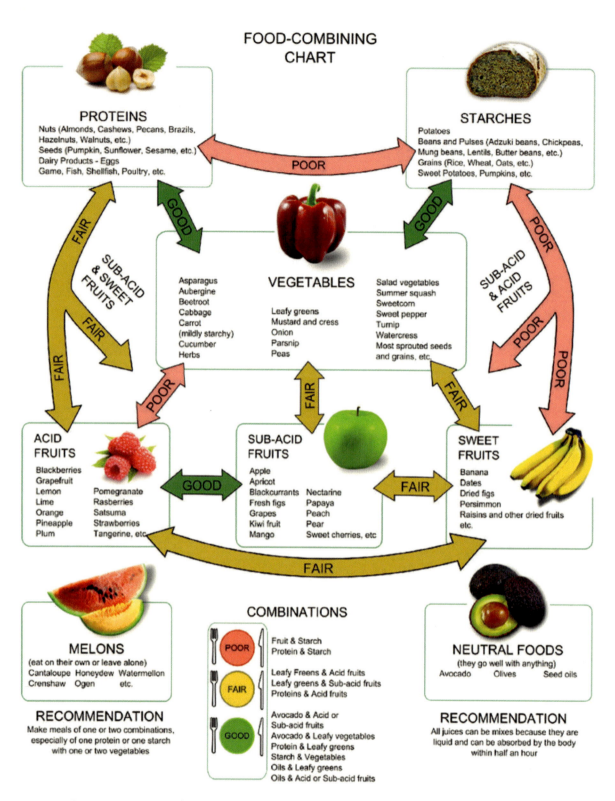

Non-starchy vegetables: (asparagus, broccoli, Brussel sprout, cabbage, celery, chard, collard greens, cucumber, eggplant, endive, green beans, kale, lettuce, parsley, spinach, sweet peppers, turnips and zucchini) are excellent if combined with mildly starchy vegetables (artichokes, beets, carrots, cauliflower, corn and peas), carbohydrates (potatoes, squash) with oily fruits (avocado, coconut). Don't eat fruit with any other food except green non-starchy vegetables.

Acid Fruits – eat these before eating other fruits

Blackberry, grapefruit, lemon, lime, orange, pineapple, strawberry, tomato

Sub-acid Fruits

Apple, apricot, blueberry, cherry, fresh fig, kiwi, mango, nectarine, papaya, peach, pear, plum

Sweet Fruits

Banana, dates, dried fruit, Thompson and Muscat grapes, dry fig, persimmon, raisin

Melons – eat with no other fruits

Watermelon, honeydew, cantaloupe

Add more or less water, or if you want to splurge, use raw coconut water. Sweet fruit contains the most calories.

For a majority of the time, my dinner is a simple carob–date–banana whip. Bananas, dates and carob provide me with enough calories. They make me feel so full that, at night, I do not binge eat. This routine has worked extremely well for me. At present, these are the most productive years—mentally, physically and emotionally—of my life.

Perhaps, you want to know what my daily routine is. I finish my last meal by 6pm, most of which is composed of my carob-date-banana whip. My next meal will be at 10am the following morning. You may find this routine a little bit on the extreme. Imagine no food intake for almost 16 hours. But I can tell you that this dining process works very well for me. This diet is calorie-, nutrient-, and glucose-rich, which allows no energy on digestion. It also helps in detoxifying and rejuvenating my body...

Remember—Food is not meant for entertainment, but for fuel.

You should understand that if you do not have sufficient calories, especially from fruits, your cravings will significantly increase for food that is not friendly to your digestive system. If we don't care about what we eat, we allow ourselves for possibilities to increase our food intake. As such, we are faced with issues we are not prepared for, like cravings for cooked food.

One of the ways to avoid binging is either a 32 oz. or 64 oz. smoothie filled with at least 6-8 bananas, 2-4 dates, a fruit of your choice and maybe some leafy greens. My ideal green is romaine or red leaf lettuce. You can always refer to the fruit combining chart, for an ideal choice. Keep in mind that it's a long journey. Do the best that you can and listen to your body!

Fruit Medley

- 1 Apple
- 1 Orange
- 1 Kiwi
- 2-lbs. Grapes
- 2-3 Dates

You can add this to a lettuce salad.

Add the fruit ingredients into a food processor, maybe with some coconut. It can be chopped up as a salad, or made into a sandwich. Place this in the blender for a smoothie or sauce. Pour it over any fruit (e.g. bananas or mangos).

This way we satisfy our cravings, eating a meal that is calorie and nutrient dense, without binging on cooked food. This, my friends, is not an easy task. It takes time to get accustomed drinking this smoothie. Do the best that you can, without beating yourself up.

Citrus Delight

- 2 Grapefruit
- 2 Oranges
- 2 Blood Oranges

Cut the fruit up into bite-sized pieces. Put it over lettuce, as a salad. Blend 2-4 bananas, 2–4 dates and ½ cup of water. Pour this mixture over fruit.

Citrus is a great juice option. Citrus is the only fruit that when juiced, the pulp or fiber remains intact. This makes it more beneficial to the body compared to other fruits that were juiced. It is great with nutrient absorption and assimilation.

> *"Say peace and be at peace, internally and externally. Prepare yourself for the next day."*
> *Fruitarians are the future. Matt Warner

Dinner is the time when your innate intelligence kicks in. Your body's continuous goal is to be in a state of peace and harmony. It doesn't want to process so many complicated foods. Eating simply is optimal.

My most ideal dinner is focused on fruit because of calories and sugar; it also aids in digestion. It is the best meal option. Mono fruit meals are the most optimal way for nourishment and rejuvenation because they are simple, rich in calories and nutrients. Mono fruit is one of the highest forms of cleansing. It is known to be extremely effective for both rejuvenation and detoxification.

Back-Up Dinner Plans

Tired of fruit, but are super hungry and afraid of binging at a local restaurant or at a fast food joint? Oily fruit to the rescue!!! Avocados, high in calories are excellent.

Spring Wake Up

- ½ cup of Zucchini
- 3-4 stalks of Celery
- ½ cup of Corn
- 2-4 Dates
- 1-2 Avocados

Use your discretion on the quantity. Do not be afraid. If you don't like an ingredient, you can always substitute with another one. Place the ingredients in the food processor and pulse.

Here are some alternatives for this recipe:

Eat it on a bed of lettuce! Or...

Eat it wrapped in a collard green! Or...

Eat plain, or blend with a squirt of lemon juice! Or...

You can eat it as a sauce or soup!

Another choice is to place the mixture in a red pepper, tomato or mushroom.

There are so many meal options, you can never be bored.

My All-Time Favorite Dish

We all have our favorite dish whether it is eaten during breakfast, lunch or dinner. Once your body is trained, you will understand that lunch is the most important time that sets the pace for the rest of the day. This is where you need your calories in bulk, to ensure that you won't binge eating at night. Weight gain is caused by not caring what you eat during the day. I choose 10 bananas in the morning hours and an avocado for lunch, so I am almost full by dinner time.

For me, this is my favorite dish for lunch.

Arnold's Guacamole

- 1½–2 Avocados
- 1 Tomato
- 2–3 stalks of Celery
- Juice of 1 Lemon

Place all of these ingredients in the food processor.

I generally eat guacamole straight up. Remember, all of your choices should be fun to eat.

Sandwich Made with No Time

Put a banana in lettuce, with some dates and enjoy. This is very simple!

I gave this sandwich to a class of 30 kids and everyone thought it was the best sandwich they ever tasted. There is no need for hot dogs when you have bananas!

For athletes, endurance and triathlon runners:

Endurance, recovery, super drink:

- 10–15 Bananas
- 10–20 Dates
- ½ blender of Water

Blend all of the ingredients. This is anywhere from 1500-3000 calories in a drink.

Sauce/Dips/Soup

Romancing the Stone

- 1 cup of Strawberries
- 3–5 Dates
- ½ cup of Water

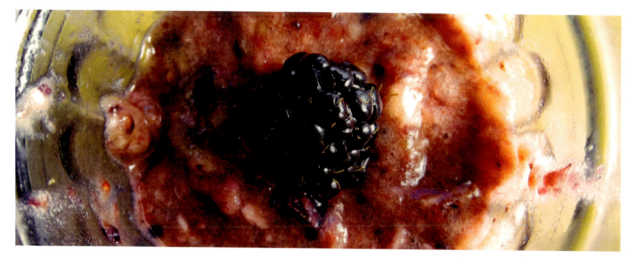

Blend the ingredients to a creamy consistency. Add more or less of each ingredient, whatever you choose.

Cut up your favorite fruit. I will always choose bananas. I pour this sauce over the bananas.

Let your imagination run wild. Any fruit will do! Any fruit can be eaten for breakfast, lunch, dinner or snack. There are so many options!

Share your new-found love of fruit and the impact it has made on your life. The body will thrive on a fruit based vegan lifestyle.

Marta's Sauce

This is dedicated to Marta, who lived with me for 30 days. Marta was diagnosed with brain tumor and has undergone a medical procedure. Her doctor said that despite the treatments done on her, she will not live much longer. It was under these circumstances that she decided to seek my advice, after having watched several of my videos on YouTube. She moved in with me for 30 days. Although she had a fairly good lifestyle of eating mostly raw vegan diet, she needed a few adjustments or fine tuning. She needed more encouragement and support, as well as a deep understanding to have a healthy lifestyle for proper healing. She needed to depend on not only herself but on a higher power, God. A year later, Marta is doing great and thriving on a LFRV lifestyle!

On this note, she began a 30-day journey with me. My focus is mostly fruit, smoothies and sometimes juices. Marta wanted sauce on her food during this journey. Hence, we made a special sauce for her vegetables, and we called it *Marta's sauce*.

Ingredients:

- 1/2 Red pepper
- 2 Sundried tomatoes
- ¼ cup of Beets
- 1–2 Dates
- 1 cup of Water

Blend all the ingredients together. Since adding fat essentially destroys the salad, we will replace it with dates.

We add dates to give the sauce more calorie and more nutrient density. Date replaces the oil which is 100% fat. When you use oil on salad, the salad jumps from 9% fat to about 70% fat with just 1 teaspoon oil.

Dips

This book is a transition book, which is geared toward people coming from a Standard American Diet. Dips have nuts and seeds, which are calorie dense. It is best to eat these meals for lunch. The dips are good with vegetables and/or salads. If eating nuts and/or seeds, it is best not to eat avocado. It is considered a double fat, having a dip combined with avocados.

Use the chart on the next page for digestive timing. Nuts and seeds should only be eaten during the hours of 12–4pm. This puts less energy on digestion. It is the key to almost every health issue.

Hummus

For whatever reason, I am addicted to hummus. In my world, I do eat some cooked foods. Hummus and cooked potatoes are my cooked foods of choice. My daughter makes a really good hummus

Ingredients:

- 8 oz. Tahini
- Juice of 1 Lemon
- 1-2 Sundried tomatoes
- ½ cup of Zucchini
- 3–4 stalks of Celery

Place all the ingredients in a food processor and pulse until smooth. Dip zucchini or cucumber in it and enjoy!

Stomach to Intestine Transit Times

Water:	10 minutes
Melon (eat it alone or leave it alone):	20 minutes
Fruits:	30-60 minutes
Vegetables:	2 hours
Starches:	3 hours
Proteins:	4 hours
Slop (everything mixed)	12 hours

Total Transit Time Comparison

Fresh, raw, properly combined foods take 12-24 hours;

However, food cooked conventionally takes 100 hours total transit time.

Stop eating on or before 6pm.

Human Circadian Rhythm

Digestion takes place from 12pm to 8pm.

Assimilation takes place from 8pm to 4am.

Elimination takes place from 4am to 12pm.

This is the natural 24-hour cycle of food processing by the human body.

Soup-to-Nuts Transition Guide to a Raw Food Diet

Ideal Diet

Soup: raw soups

Fruit: all whole to juice fresh produce or unsulfured dried fruit (ideally with some water)

Vegetables: All raw vegetables

No meat, fish dairy or grains

Sweets: dates, raisins, dried figs

Beverages: freshly extracted vegetable and fruit juice and filtered or distilled water

Transitional Diet

Soups: soups made from scratch without fat stock or salt

Fruit: stewed and unsweetened fresh or frozen fruit

Vegetables: raw, baked or cooked vegetables (fresh or frozen)

No meat, fish or dairy

Grains: whole grain cereals, gluten free products (e.g. pasta, bread), brown rice, millet, grain sprouts

Foods to Avoid

Soup: canned or powdered soups

Fruit: canned and sweetened fruits, commercial raisins

Vegetables: canned vegetables, fried potatoes and other fried vegetables, corn and potato chips

All meat

Fish: all fish, clams, oysters, shrimp, lobster

Dairy: all dairy products such as whipped toppings, milk, cheese, eggs and ice cream

Ideal Diet

Seasonings: Used for seasonings should be herbs, and dried vegetables (e.g. celery, tomatoes), fruit sauces (e.g. tamarind sauce), seaweed vegetables

Nuts and seeds: raw cashews, almonds, walnuts, and sunflower seeds in small amounts (no more than a handful, a few times a week), Low-fat seeds are acceptable (e.g. chia seeds, buckwheat)

Transitional Diet

Sweets: stevia, raw, unfiltered honey, rice syrup, unsulfured molasses, carob, pure maple syrup (use sparingly)

Beverages: herbal teas (non-caffeine), cereal coffees, organic bottled juice

Oils: cold pressed canola and sunflower oil, cold pressed vegan mayo

Seasoning: Onions, Braggs Liquid Aminos

Nuts and seeds: raw nuts and seeds in small amounts

Foods to Avoid

Grains: wheat and bleached flour products, pasta, crackers, white rice, cold cereal

Sweets: refined white and brown sugar, syrup, chocolate, gum, cake, cookies, donuts, pies

Beverages: soft drinks, alcohol, coffee, tea, cocoa, artificial fruit drinks, canned juice, caffeine

Oils: hydrogenated oil, butter, margarine, lard, shortening

Seasonings: salt, pepper, vinegar

Nuts and seeds: peanuts, peanut butter, roasted seeds and nuts

Nuts are funny

In understanding dips, nuts, which we use extensively in our café, are considered transitory meal options. This means nuts are better than meat. They are rich in calories and fat, however, they lack nutrients, dense and harder to digest than veggies and fruits. This is key to healing fully—if your fat content is high and the nutrient density is low.

In my world, I keep nuts to a minimum. I only recommend a handful of nuts, a few times a week. The reason I recommend this is because nuts have a fat content of 70-80% by volume. This makes it difficult for the body to process. This leaves less energy focused on healing, as the body is putting out more energy to process the fats. Unfortunately, many restaurants, including vegan restaurants, focus on high-fat options, with the food cooked in oils and butter. However, they taste good, yet do not do any good on the body.

In the initial phases of a transition to a raw vegan lifestyle, when the focus is on entertainment, nuts have a place. As time goes on, the importance of nuts will be less and less as we begin listening to the body's language and the importance of giving it the best choices for healing and rejuvenation!

Soups

Soups are fun and easy, with nothing to think about when preparing. You can make soups easily by using the blender. When making soups with the blender, the nutrients are more easily absorbed when consumed, as well as assimilated and digested. Unlike juicing, soup contains all of the fiber from the ingredients. Thus, more nutrients are available.

Mushroom Soup

- 8 medium-large Button Mushrooms
- 1/2 stalk celery
- 10 raisins or 1 date
- 1/4 of an avocado, or more for creaminess
- Squeeze of lemon juice
- Optional: Small slice of ginger or small clove garlic
- 1/2 cup water

Place all of the ingredients into the blender, and blend until a creamy consistency is achieved. Add water if needed.

Gazpacho

- Tomatoes
- Celery
- Red Pepper
- Zucchini
- Lemon
- Cilantro
- Optional: add ginger

Add ingredients to the blender, along with the water. I personally don't measure the ingredients. Keep in mind today's likes may be tomorrow's dislikes. It's all part of the journey.

If there is no oil, salt or fat, there will be very minimal calories. I recommend this for lunch, with a heavier meal that has avocado or nuts. The other option is at dinner time, provided, of course, you met your caloric needs. If caloric needs are not met, add avocado so that you do not binge eating at night.

Remember the 5'S theory. You can turn this into a salad, with avocado added. Or blend with a small amount of water and sundried tomatoes, to use this as a sauce. You can pour this over your salad.

Rich Green Soup

This is considered a meal, because of the fat content. It is also calorie rich. This recipe has avocados and pumpkin seeds, which add up as a double fat. A double fat is not ideal; however, it is better than the conventional food out there. Blending them together allows for better food absorption. This is ideal for lunch time, because of the caloric density of avocado and pumpkin seeds.

Ingredients:

- Avocado
- Broccoli
- Pumpkin Seeds
- Zucchini
- Lemon Juice
- Water

Place all the ingredients in the blender. As with other recipes in this book, it can be made into various meal types. Substitute this soup for a salad, if you'd like. The ingredients can be blended and put on top of a bed of lettuce.

Also, the ingredients can be pulsed in the food processor, and can be made into sandwiches or wraps using nori, collard greens or lettuce.

Soup Option

Soup is just a blend away from a meal. The hardest part is not being entertained by the food, and seeing it as a fuel source. If you are in a healing crisis, soup can become essential due to liquid minerals. The hardest part is focusing on the vegetables. Salt, ginger and garlic are irritants. This means more harm is done than good when adding these to the soup. Adding oil to the soup increases the fat content significantly. What was once a low-fat soup becomes a high-fat soup because of the addition of oil!

The other side of soup is enjoying the spices, the oils, the ginger, the garlic, the what-have-you's.

Cream of Tomato Soup

- 3 Tomatoes
- 3 Sundried Tomatoes
- 2 Dates
- 1 cup of Water

Place all of the ingredients into the blender, and blend until a creamy consistency is achieved.

Carrot Dream

- 2 Carrots
- 1/2 of a small Beet
- 2 stalks of Celery
- 1/2 of a Cucumber
- 1/2 cup of Water

Place all the ingredients into a blender, and enjoy.

When making the soups, select the colored fruits and vegetables that you most resonate with. You can also let the soup blends for a slightly longer period of time, to achieve a warmer temperature. If you are looking for a denser meal, just add some nuts, seeds or avocados.

Snacks and in-between

On a typical day...

I carry a bunch of bananas and an avocado. These are my go to foods. I go to the supermarket to buy packaged fruit, such as berries or watermelon. I make the best choices when I eat out. I always choose vegan foods. I enjoy my day, without worries and without fear! I consider myself a fruitarian (as opposed to vegetarian). My daily caloric intake is 65–85% from fruits.

Breakdown

15 bananas:	1600 calories
2 avocados:	500 calories
2-4 oz. dates:	200 calories
Total:	2300 calories

My daily caloric intake is easily reached when I make a big container of green smoothie in the morning, with sufficient calories!

7–8 bananas:	800 calories
1 apple:	80 calories
1 pear:	80 calories
2 oz. dates:	120 calories
Total:	1080 calories

I occasionally enjoy cooked food, but I choose those I am okay with. I love eating hummus or potatoes of any kind. Everything happens for a reason and that's part of a learning experience. My body can tell me, in no uncertain terms if it is overloaded. I know because I keep on coughing or sneezing. When that happens, I immediately back to an all-fruit diet. Doing so, my body can catch up, heal and rejuvenate to operate more efficiently.

In conclusion...

Every moment is a moment of love.

Enjoy my book!
Conquer your fear!
You cannot make a mistake!
Eat your fruit and vegetables!
Love yourself unconditionally.

Arnold's Day-In, Day-Out Secrets to a Healthy Lifestyle

These are the highlights of what a typical day is like for me and what I shoot for on a daily basis.

Set goals of intention

I want to stay young without aches and pains and to have a young spirit enabling me to live the dream. I want to feel the sunshine, dance to the beat of music and focus on my youthful appearance. My mantra is to be a lean, mean fighting machine. I live and breathe this mantra to lead a lifestyle eating fruits and greens which eventually comes 90% of my calorie needs. I generally eat cooked food two to three times a week in the form of potatoes or grains. I eat potatoes with vegetables on social occasions. Other times, I'll indulge in a grain meal once or twice a week. These are my tools to maintain my eternal youth.

Even at 69, I continue to move into greater levels of fitness and optimal health. I read, study and try whatever resonates with me the most. I tend to stick to a lifestyle eat mostly fruits and leafy greens with a daily exercise routine outlined in this chapter.

Focus on what is working

This is the real deal. You alone would know better what works and what doesn't work for you. In my experience, living on a diet of mostly fruits and leafy greens truly works. The secret is to eat a significant amount of fruit, anywhere from 15 to 25 pieces a day. If I am not able to eat this amount of fruits, I would probably get into eating more gourmet food. But be forewarned though, gourmet food is rich in heavy oil and nuts. I feel my best when I'm living on high-calorie fruits and low nut, oil and spice intake.

Exercise daily

A daily routine of exercise helps me achieve my mantra of being a lean, mean machine. I have learned over the years that morning is the best time for a workout. I do a combination of stretching, strength training and aerobic exercises from 30 to 120 minutes. I generally opt to take on one exercise that is a little bit out of my comfort zone. For example, I'm learning how to walk hand over hand across an 8-foot beam. It may be simple for some people to do, but I'm finding it hard to do at the moment. I don't exercise at night because I need to consume a lot of calories after I work out. It would throw my whole routine out of balance if I worked out in the evening.

Write down and review your life goals periodically

A lot of what I do is about me, how big my ego is, and what I am willing to do to maintain my daily routine. My major goal is to be happy. I'm willing to do everything to create a purpose and unity in my actions and words. I want to be in a state of love—with those I know and even with people I do not know. My wish is to be like a ship that sails on the smooth water. That, to me, is the key.

I encourage you to define what you want to achieve, write it down, look at it each morning and then BE the things you really want to be, day in and day out.

Eat enough calories to maintain your body weight (weight multiplied by 10)

This is one of the many random statements I make about meeting caloric needs. The basic metabolism rate to get the right amount of calories is based on how many calories are required to be expended. If one did absolutely nothing but lay in bed the whole day and then went to sleep, the amount of calories expended would comprise one's basic metabolic rate. The formula is to take your weight and multiply it by 10 to establish your weight calorie requirement. In my case, my weight calorie requirement would be 140 pounds x 10 = 1440 calories a day.

If I were living a sedentary lifestyle, I would add 400-600 calories. If I had a very active lifestyle, then I would add 800-100 calories. In my case, I need about 2200-2500 calories a day. I don't count calories, but I do have a base that I shoot for. I don't keep any food at home. I eat five to seven bananas after my morning workout. As soon as I get to work, I make a green smoothie with about 10 bananas and 1 head of romaine lettuce. Generally, I drink this smoothie, which is about 48-64 ounces, in 4-12 oz. increments throughout the day. I like to consume 40-60% of my caloric requirement from bananas. That's about 1000 calories. I also try to have 10 pieces of dates, approximately 55 calories a piece, along with celery to add more greens into each day's regimen. I generally eat 1.5 avocados to meet my fat requirements.

Using that as my foundation, if I stick to this program, by nighttime I am satiated for the day. I don't feel deprived in any way and have no desire to stray from this eating plan. Then I do my dry fasting three or four days a week from 6pm or 7pm until 10am the following morning. I have been on this routine since the spring of 2012.

Dry fasting means no food or water, during this 12–16 hour period.

Rebound three to four times a week

Rebounding has been my rock exercise for over 20 years. Rebound exercise (or "Rebounding") is a type of elastically leveraged low-impact exercise usually performed on a device known as a rebounder—sometimes called a "mini-trampoline. I literally live and die by this form of exercise as my foundation before anything else. The main reason I enjoy doing this exercise and strongly advocate for it is that it helps keep the lymphatic system moving, thereby boosting the immune system. Doing this exercise keeps the body young.

Rebounding works on three levels:

- Acceleration: upward motion
- Deceleration: downward motion
- Gravitational: downward pull

When these three levels are joined in a single jump, the lymph system begins a pumping action to remove all water that surrounds each cell. When this happens, the immune system has more room to move, and when it moves, it will attack any cell that is not part of the body, especially cancer cells. These cancer cells are destroyed by one immune fighter, in particular, the T8 Cell, which contains hydrogen peroxide. This agent kills all cancer cells that it zaps.

Drink lemon juice and water

If you are drinking water, add lemon juice, this one step is extremely beneficial for the body. Drinking lemon juice is very alkalizing and raises the pH of the blood, and it starts the small intestine's peristalsis movement. Drink as much of it as you desire.

Earn your breakfast

This is a big one for me. I believe one can't eat until he or she has earned it. This is the reason why I exercise from about 6:30am to 8:30am. I can't imagine living any other way than starting my daily routine with exercise, loving every moment of it, and eating mostly fruits and leafy vegetables for the rest of the day. Doing this keeps me steady on a smooth climb to complete nirvana. I love, thrive and am complete on this routine. Every moment is a blessed moment.

I have eight to ten different routines that I complete. I do a little of cardio exercise, a little of strength training, a little of resistance exercise and any exercise that pushes me out of my comfort zone. I incorporate as many different kinds of exercise into my routine as possible. I have a mantra of four words that is embedded in my soul as I go about my day. This mantra drives me daily, monthly, and yearly to maintain my youth, my stamina, and help me be a light for others. These words are "lean mean fighting machine".

I used to exercise in the evening, but couldn't get enough calories to maintain my weight. Exercising at night doesn't work for me because, in my experience, when one eats after an exercise session, this activity causes the digestive system to work harder than usual, causing nerve energy to become depleted. Digestion needs energy to break down, assimilate, and transport nutrients to wherever they need to go. When I exercise at night, it adversely impacted my sleeping and bodily restoration process. Needless to say, I don't exercise at night anymore.

Eat only fruits — or fruits and greens in green smoothies — until noon

This is a big one for me because after working out I am starved. What works for me is eating five to seven bananas, a supersize 64 oz. green smoothie with 10 bananas, a head of romaine and maybe 1 oz. of dates too. The reason I suggest eating fruits until noon is that the body is programmed by something called the circadian rhythm, which is from about 4am until noon. The body enters an elimination process, cleaning out all the debris and toxic matter that accumulated the previous day. To benefit the body during this process, keep digestive energy to a minimum. This is easily obtained by eating fruit juices or a calorie and nutrient rich fruit or green smoothie that does not tax the digestive system.

Eat enough calories

One of the hardest things to maintain is eating enough calories. The body needs a certain amount of calories to survive and thrive. Most foods served, sold, bought and eaten is calorie rich, yet nutrient poor. To thrive, we need to have calories and nutrients. Vegetables have very few calories and are low in glucose, which is abundant in fruits. Therefore, fruits should be the major source of calories and nutrients. Eating the greatest amount of our calorie intake between 10am to 5pm, will satiate our appetites and give the body enough calories. You won't be hungry by dinner time. Dinner should comprise a low-calorie meal of fruits or vegetables, and this meal should be ideally completed by 7pm, or 3 hours before going to bed.

Eat your fat at lunch

I am a firm believer in a low-fat regimen, as per the 80-10-10 dietary program prescribed by Dr. Doug Graham. It clearly states that a high-fat diet is the major cause of most diseases. High fat not only blocks the uptake of nutrients but clogs the arteries, slowing the transport of and making it impossible to deliver nutrients to the cell. This means fat is harsh on the body for processing. In an ideal world, it is best to eat fat at lunch because according to our built-in circadian rhythm elimination takes place from 4am until noon. And this is the reason also why fruits are best consumed in the morning. Digestion begins at noon, the best time to eat your heavy meal for calories and fuel, and to give the body enough time to properly digest all food. Assimilation is from 8pm to 4am when the body begins to absorb all the food taken in during the day. This is the time to stop eating, so you won't interfere with your body's natural healing, cleansing, and recharging processes.

Drink 32 oz. of green smoothies every day

Believe it or not, drinking 32 oz. of green smoothies a day is the secret to staying raw for the majority of people who begin a raw vegan lifestyle. I've been giving classes on raw food with an emphasis on fruits for more than 10 years. In all these years, and for thousands of people whom I have taught lessons in raw foods and natural hygiene, only a handful of students were able to stay raw for any length of time. Why? Because this lifestyle approach is just too foreign and "extreme", and not culturally favorable. In most cases, most people could not continue their raw lifestyles. But with the introduction of the green smoothie, it generally works. Green smoothie has been my salvation, so as to most people to whom I have taught a raw food lifestyle.

Green smoothies are easy to make. Just put all the ingredients into the blender, add water and presto — you're done! Green smoothies also taste great! By adding fruits and leafy greens together, with an emphasis on bananas and dates, they have almost the nutritional value of mother's milk, wow!

Green smoothies are nutrient and calorie rich! In our society today, most prepared food is calorie rich but nutrient deficient. This is because as soon as you cook food above 105 degrees, you destroy the life force of the food. While on the other hand, green smoothies are loaded with goodness! This is the secret that makes the whole raw foods regimen work!

A Basic Recipe for a Green Smoothie

This recipe makes 32 ounces. Drink at least two 16 ounce servings a day.

- 2 bananas
- 1 pear
- 1 apple
- 1 ounce of dates
- 2-4 leaves of greens (kale, collard, romaine, etc. Alternate throughout the week)
- 16 ounces of water and love!

Eat fruits or vegetables for dinner

In my opinion, dinner should be the least toxic load on your digestive system. Most fruits are mostly water, taking less than an hour to go from the stomach to the intestines. This time-frame also enables the body to have sufficient energy to detoxify and rejuvenate what needs to be repaired first in the body. The same holds true for vegetables. The secret is getting most of your calorie requirements from 10am–5pm so that dinner calorie requirements won't be as great. When this regimen is followed, you are ready for the important stage of sleep to restore your nerve energy. The body is fully prepared to do this while expending minimal energy on digestion.

When to stop eating

This thought process goes along with fasting and the Seven Steps to Optimum Health. If the last meal is either fruits or vegetables, which take minimal time to digest, the body, in its infinite wisdom, will continually move toward homeostasis and rebalancing the system from the minutest organism to the most complex. I suggest that all eating ideally stops between 6 and 7 pm. The following morning, eat your first meal—fruit only after 6 am. By not eating during these hours, your body has hours of body repair and rejuvenation and stimulating detoxification. This is one of the major secrets for staying fit, young and ageless.

Open a window

Our bodies need a continual flow of fresh air and sunshine. When we deny our body the earth's life force, we deny ourselves a major source of fuel that our bodies require. In the summer, many stay inside all day in an air-conditioned environment. The recirculated dead air loaded with microorganisms can wreak havoc on the body's immune system. If we stay indoors most of the time during winter, we suffer from colds and flu because we aren't getting sufficient fresh air or sunshine. In my opinion, if either of these seasonal factors bother you, at the very least keep your windows open.

Go to bed early

Sleep is the body's built-in battery, enabling the body to be in a constant state of renewable energy. Sleep is the power force that keeps all of the body's processes moving. If the body desperately needs to recharge and you forcefully try to keep it awake, there is absolutely no contest. The body will win. The most effective time to go to sleep is two to three hours after dinner, meaning 9:30pm to 11pm when our digestive energy is quiet and the darkness calls our souls to lie down, close our eyes and become one with sleep. Our bodies are aligned to sleep when the sun sets and awaken when the sun rises. Our bodies have this innate wisdom for perfection and optimum health. Sleep is the cornerstone for creating fire that ignites our souls.

Don't beat yourself up

Life is a long, long journey with many ups and downs, curveballs and home runs. Each challenge represents a beautiful part of the ride. We have to be gracious and accept the flow of life. One of my favorite quotes is *"how is this to my benefit and what can I learn from this experience?"* This means you can take a negative experience and quickly change it into a positive one. Realize that all thoughts and feelings that suck the life out of us because of negative interpretations can be quickly changed in any given moment to sunshine thoughts.

These are my 17 day-by-day steps, I strive for on a daily basis. These are my daily rituals, which keep me on a continual vacation and enable me to thrive, not just survive. I want to live a life of purpose and not get bogged down by a daily life routine. I feel that at 69, my life is just beginning on all levels. I am sharing with the readers my experience out of humility and gratitude. I invite you, my friends, to learn or discard the information I'm providing here as you see fit. The choice is yours.

Tips from Marisa Angela

Marisa Angela is a life coach and co-producer of my newest documentary. She is also a supporter of self-empowerment. Marisa shares her daily routine.

Marisa Angela's Approach to Optimal Health

When you have an ailment that you want to heal, you need to approach it from ALL angles; not just one. Here are 13 simple routine changes you can make TODAY that are not diet related:

- Posture for lumbar support
- Sleep on left side (for better digestion)
- Castor Oil Packs
- Brush teeth with Bentonite Clay (Earth Paste)
- Daily meditation (because stress is highly acidic)
- Dry brush skin
- Use ceramic knives (to prevent food oxidation)
- Change light bulbs in home/workplace to 5000k
- No sunglasses (the brain needs a full spectrum of light)
- No bras (lymph drainage is prevented)
- Bless your food and drinks–it changes their molecular structure (look up Dr. Masaru Emoto)
- Oil pull
- Go to bed at sunset (to regulate cortisol & circadian rhythms)

Don Bennett's Optimal Health Tips

From Don Bennett, disease avoidance specialist (D.A.S.), one of my heroes whose book 'Avoiding Degenerative Disease' is one of my primary go-to references. I love this book and love Don Bennett's information. The knowledge he has is at the top of the line, which I resonate with. Here are some of his tips.

Take-home points from...

How to Have the BEST Odds of Avoiding Degenerative Disease

A lecture by Don Bennett, DAS

You're not likely to get a chronic degenerative disease unless you're doing the things that cause it. Vibrant health is your natural state and is eroded by unnatural lifestyle practices.

It is vital that you pay equal attention to all the 'basics of health' if you want to live to your health and longevity potentials… human diet, physical activity, being properly hydrated, enough sunshine, enough deep sleep, enough stress management and laughter, toxin avoidance, mis- and dis-information avoidance.

Overeating is caused by attempting to satisfy the body's desire for nutrients, which results from eating food that is nutritionally lacking.

Healthier diet = easier digestion = more energy and less disease.

The difference between 10% (left over basal metabolism and digestion) and 30% is a 200% increase (an unhealthy diet requires about 60% of the daily energy available for digestion, and a healthy human diet requires about 40%).

Joint pain, heartburn, headache, low energy, allergies, low sex drive, can't sleep, congestion, etc. are all symptoms of an underlying problem… they are NOT the problem. Resolve the problem and the symptoms of the problem vanish; deal with the symptoms of the problem and the problem itself remains and gets worse. For the most part, modern health-care deals with the relief of symptoms, and is reactive in nature as opposed to preventive.

The above points are expanded upon in the book, *How to Have the Best Odds of Avoiding Degenerative Disease.*

Visit health101.org.

Credits

Arnold Kauffman Recipe Book

Published December 2016

For more information of our titles, please visit www.arnoldsway.com or search for Arnold Kauffman on Amazon.com

We welcome feedback at arnoldsway@yahoo.com

Author: Arnold N. Kauffman

Arnold N. Kauffman is the Author of

Healing Success Stories from Arnold's Way

The Way of Arnold: Experiencing Your Full Potential While Turning Back the Clock With Every Loving Raw Moment

Arnold's Way Childproof Recipes For Everyone

All the Many Ways of Arnold

Why Johnny Nucell Feels So Good

Seven-Point-Seven: Segue to Energetic Health

Editor: Drew Martin

Images: Smilewithyourheart.com

Tapintoheaven.com

Livingforce.ca

Photography: Caitlyn Kennedy Photography

Production: Electric Publishing

You Don't Want to Miss a Beat!

To receive the latest updates, a monthly newsletter, in-store specials, and the best free content on the web on health, wellness, and diet find Arnold's Way on

YouTube

Instagram

Facebook

& Twitter

You can now sign up for the free monthly newsletter online at www.arnoldsway.com

Made in the USA
Middletown, DE
22 June 2022